FOOD BRANDS WE LOVE

McDONALD'S

By Kaitlyn Duling

Kaleidoscope
Minneapolis, MN

The Quest for Discovery Never Ends

This edition is co-published by agreement between Kaleidoscope and World Book, Inc.

Kaleidoscope Publishing, Inc.
6012 Blue Circle Drive
Minnetonka, MN 55343 U.S.A.

World Book, Inc.
180 North LaSalle St., Suite 900
Chicago IL 60601 U.S.A.

Kaleidoscope ISBNs
978-1-64519-214-5 (library bound)
978-1-64519-282-4 (ebook)

World Book ISBN
978-0-7166-4192-6 (library bound)

Library of Congress Control Number
2020936218

Developed and produced by Focus Strategic Communications Inc.

Printed in the United States of America.

Bigfoot lurks within one of the images in this book. It's up to you to find him!

TABLE OF
CONTENTS

Chapter 1

Real Food, Real Fast

Ben and his mom sat across from each other. They shared some French fries. Ben chewed his hamburger while Mom sipped a shake. The two knew they were having a yummy lunch. What they didn't know was that the same scene was unfolding all across the world. The "golden arches" of McDonald's crisscross Earth.

FUN FACT

Donald Gorske holds the record for most Big Macs ever eaten. He has eaten over 30,000 Big Macs since 1972. Donald eats two Big Macs a day.

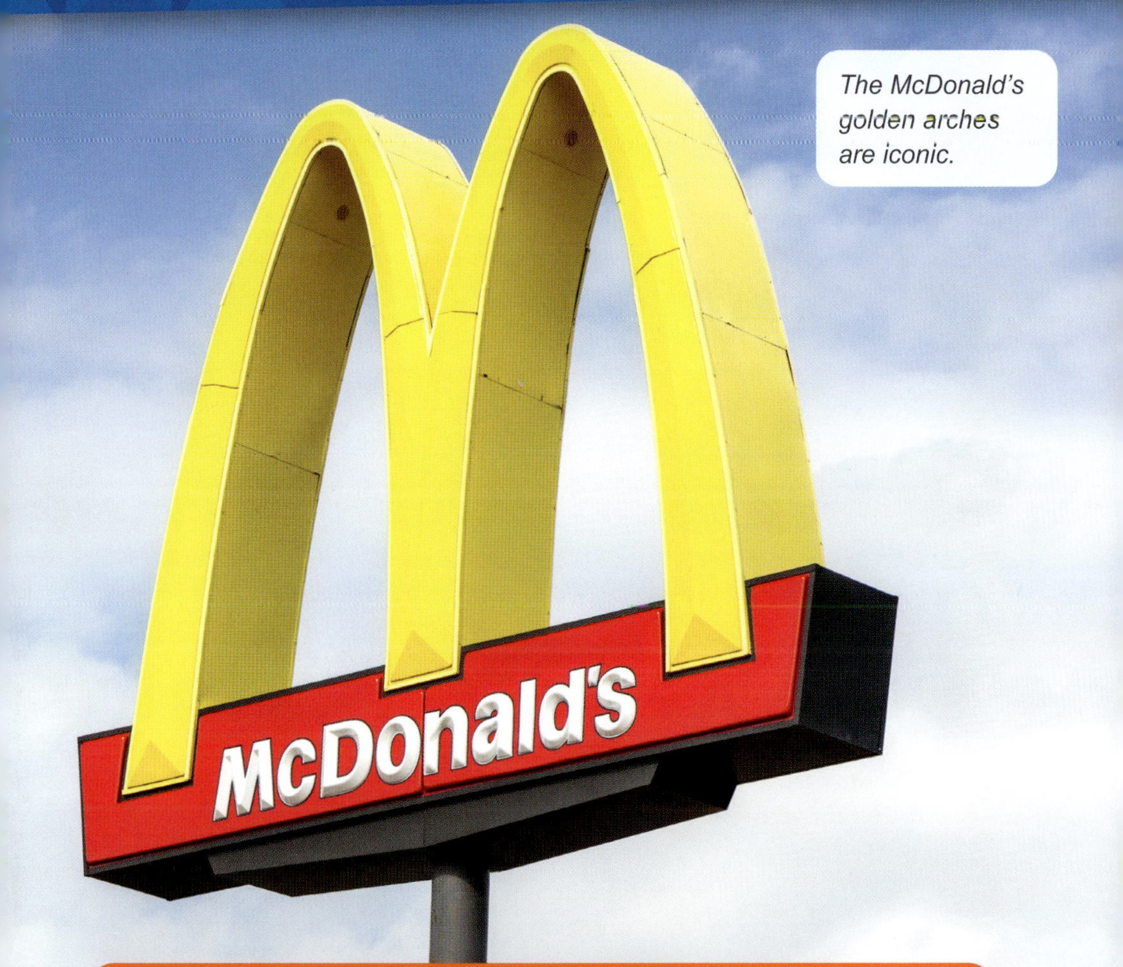

The McDonald's golden arches are iconic.

McDonald's fries are a tasty treat.

Chicken McNuggets are one of the most popular McDonald's menu items.

McDonald's is famous for its **affordable** menu. Some items are just $1 or $2. The restaurant has food and drinks for every meal of the day. Egg McMuffins are tasty at breakfast. An iced coffee from McCafé is an afternoon treat. And the Big Mac will fill you up at dinnertime. Ben and his mom stopped by when they were in a hurry. McDonald's was one of the first **fast food** restaurants. Customers receive their food just minutes after ordering. When you're hungry, fast food is a quick and easy option.

FUN FACT

Chicken McNuggets are made in only four shapes. Their names are bone, bell, ball, and boot. They are designed for dipping.

There are 14,000 McDonald's restaurants in the US. That's an average of nearly 300 in every state. The company employs nearly 2 million people. Some celebrities have worked at McDonald's. Rachel McAdams, P!nk, and Lin-Manuel Miranda all worked for the company at some point.

Ben stirred his McFlurry. He thought about working at McDonald's someday. Maybe he could fry the French fries. Or he could wear a headset and take orders from the cars at the drive-thru window. At a McDonald's drive-thru, food is usually delivered in less than five minutes. If he worked hard, Ben could even own a McDonald's restaurant. Then he could eat Chicken McNuggets for breakfast, lunch, and dinner. What could be better?

Drive-Thrus allow people to get McDonald's while staying in their cars.

Chapter 2

History of McDonald's

It feels like McDonald's has been around forever. But the **brand** is barely 75 years old. The first McDonald's was started by two brothers. Mac and Dick McDonald grew up in New Hampshire and moved to California. There, in 1948, they put all of their hopes and dreams into a restaurant. They sold burgers for just 15 cents. The first McDonald's was a drive-in. Customers ate the burgers, shakes, and fries in their cars. The food was delivered by **carhops**.

FUN FACT

McDonald's first mascot was a chef named Speedee. His face was shaped like a hamburger. Speedee was replaced by Ronald McDonald in 1963.

Dick McDonald enjoys the 50 billionth McDonald's hamburger.

McDonald's used to look very different.

Six years later, the brothers met Ray Kroc. He sold milkshake machines. Kroc saw great possibilities in the business. Their restaurants featured fast service and good food. They quickly became a success. Kroc taught the brothers about **franchising**. With this agreement, restaurant owners use McDonald's name and ideas. They also sell McDonald's food. But McDonald's doesn't own the actual restaurant.

McDonald's franchises spread across the US. Americans loved the burgers and fries. The brand was a hit. In 1961, Kroc bought the entire company for $2.7 million.

Ray Kroc

CONDIMENT CONTROVERSY

At the first McDonald's, customers couldn't get ketchup with their fries. It was served with hamburgers only. Finally, after years of complaints, the company responded. They introduced small "dunk cups" for ketchup. Ketchup packets weren't added until 1968.

Ray Kroc had big goals. He wanted to build 1,000 McDonald's. After he built those, he wanted 1,000 more. Today, there are more than 36,000 McDonald's. No matter where you travel, you are likely to find one. The brand has grown well beyond its founders' dreams.

Sleek looking McCafés are popular now.

McDONALD'S BRAND TIMELINE

1948
Mac and Dick McDonald open the original McDonald's restaurant.

1955
The first McDonald's franchise opens.

1963
Ronald McDonald is introduced.

1968
McDonald's rolls out the Big Mac.

1948 1955 1961 1963 1965 1967 1968

1967
McDonald's expands into Canada and Puerto Rico.

1961
Ray Kroc buys the McDonald's Corporation from the McDonald brothers for $2.7 million.

1965
The Filet-O-Fish becomes the first new item added to the national menu.

1954
Ray Kroc visits McDonald's and convinces the brothers to open a franchise.

1972
Egg McMuffins are invented.

1974
The first Ronald McDonald House is founded.

1983
Chicken McNuggets are made available nationwide.

1993
The world's first McCafé opens in Australia.

2017
McDonald's begins testing a vegan hamburger.

1972 1979 1983 1988 1993 2015 2017 2020

1988
10,000 McDonald's restaurants are in operation.

2020
A new breakfast item is rolled out nationwide: the McChicken Biscuit.

1979
Happy Meals make their first appearance.

2015
McDonald's launches All Day Breakfast in the US.

Chapter 3
Fun on the Menu

Alex couldn't stop smiling. His stomach was growling, but he didn't mind. He was on his way to McDonald's. Nothing could ruin his day.

Ever since he could remember, Alex had ordered Happy Meals at McDonald's. The kids' meals were first introduced in 1979. Since then, they haven't changed much. Alex loved to open up the red cardboard box. He would find a hamburger and fries inside. His favorite part was the toy. Happy Meals were made just for kids. When they grow up, those kids still remember the fun of a Happy Meal. Many of the toys have become **collector's items**.

Happy Meal toys sometimes come from popular kids movies.

McDonald's PlayPlaces are a lot of fun.

Alex finished his milk and apple slices. Then he got ready to play. Many McDonald's restaurants are home to PlayPlaces. The first was built in the mid-1970s. The outdoor playground was filled with McDonald's characters. In the 1990s, the playgrounds moved inside. The tubes and slides were safer for kids.

FUN FACT

Over the years, McDonald's has created tons of popular characters. Grimace, Hamburglar, Birdie the Early Bird, and Mayor McCheese are just a few.

Ronald McDonald helps make kids feel better.

Ronald McDonald Houses are usually right by hospitals.

Alex knew he was lucky. Some kids aren't healthy enough to play. That's why, in 1974, McDonald's created a **nonprofit** organization to help sick kids and their families. When kids are in the hospital, their families can stay at a Ronald McDonald House. The free service provides meals and beds. It helps families stick together and save money.

KIDS' MEALS...FOR ADULTS?

In 1997, McDonald's introduced a Happy Meal toy that turned the world upside-down. The "Teenie Beanie Baby" toys were extremely popular with adults. McDonald's sold about 100 million Happy Meals in just two weeks. Some adults even said they threw the food away. They thought the toys would be valuable someday.

Chapter 4
Going Global

Kaya bit into a crispy French fry. It was salty and hot. Kaya had always loved McDonald's fries. She loved to eat them at home in Chicago, IL. She ate them on vacation in Orlando, FL. And now she was eating them in Paris, France. French fries in France—delicious.

McDonald's restaurants may look a little different around the world, but they always have the golden arches.

FUN FACT

In 2012, a McNugget was sold on eBay for about $8,100. What was so special about it? The McNugget looked like George Washington.

There are thousands of McDonald's across the globe. Almost everyone knows the McDonald's **logo**. No matter where they travel, customers can always order their favorites. McNuggets, fries, and Big Macs are standard menu items.

Poutine is French Canadian food.

McDonald's also builds its menu to suit local tastes. Some items are available only in certain countries. In Canada, fries can be topped with gravy and cheese. This is called poutine. In Singapore, guests

eat curly fries. Instead of ketchup, the fries are dipped into **curry** sauce. The meal ends with a sweet coconut pie.

Some menus are unique. A favorite fry topping in Japan? Fish eggs. Diners in India can trade their beef burger for a potato patty. The dish is called the McAloo Tikki Burger. "Aloo" means "potato."

The McAloo Tikki Burger is vegetarian.

Balloon bouquets and apple pie cakes make for a very McHappy wedding.

Finally, couples in Hong Kong have a unique way to show their McDonald's pride. There, fans can have their weddings at McDonald's. The McDonald's Wedding Party features a "cake" made out of Apple Pie boxes. The bride's flowers are made of balloons. And every guest takes home a Happy Meal toy. Now that is a meal worth traveling for.

McDONALD'S ON THE MOUNTAIN

Since 1996, skiers in Sweden have been able to visit a ski-thru restaurant. "McSki" is located in Lindvallen, a popular ski resort. Skiers just glide up to the window and place their order. There's no need to remove their gear.

AT-HOME

FRENCH FRIES RECIPE

Note: Do not do this alone. Make sure an adult is helping.

INGREDIENTS:

- 4 starchy potatoes, such as Russet or Yukon Gold potatoes
- ¼ cup cooking oil, such as vegetable oil
- Cooking spray
- 2 tsp salt
- ½ tsp of other spices you like, such as onion powder, garlic powder, paprika, or pepper. It's up to you!

DIRECTIONS:

1. Peel and rinse potatoes.
2. Cut the potatoes into ½-inch-wide sticks. Fries bake better when they are all the same size.
3. Place the sticks into a bowl of cold water and let them soak for 30 minutes.
4. Drain and pat the sticks dry.
5. Preheat the oven to 425°F and line a sheet pan with foil. Coat the foil with cooking spray.
5. Place the potato sticks in a large bowl with the oil, salt, and other spices. Stir until the sticks are completely coated.
5. Spread the sticks in a single layer on the baking sheet. Bake for 30-35 minutes or until golden brown. Enjoy!

BEYOND THE BOOK

After reading the book, it's time to think about what you learned. Try the following exercises to jumpstart your ideas.

THINK

THAT'S NEWS TO ME. McDonald's has a complicated history. Consider how you learn about foods and brands. What information can be found in news articles? What about news programs on TV? Where can you go to find news you can trust?

CREATE

PRIMARY SOURCES. Primary sources provide firsthand accounts of an event. Interviews, videos, and photographs are all examples of primary sources. Create a list of the kinds of primary sources you might be able to find about McDonald's.

SHARE

WHAT'S YOUR OPINION? The text states that McDonald's is famous for its affordable menu. Do you agree with that statement? Provide evidence from the text to support your opinion. Share your position and evidence with a friend. Does your friend find the argument convincing?

GROW

DRAWING CONNECTIONS. Create a diagram that shows and explains connections between Ray Kroc and McDonald's. How does learning about the history help you better understand food brands?

RESEARCH NINJA

Visit *www.ninjaresearcher.com/2145* to learn how to take your research skills and book report writing to the next level.

RESEARCH

DIGITAL LITERACY TOOLS

SEARCH LIKE A PRO
Learn how to use search engines to find useful websites.

FACT OR FAKE?
Discover how you can tell a trusted website from an untrustworthy resource.

TEXT DETECTIVE
Explore how to zero in on the information you need most.

SHOW YOUR WORK
Research responsibly—learn how to cite sources.

WRITE

GET TO THE POINT
Learn how to express your main ideas.

PLAN OF ATTACK
Learn prewriting exercises and create an outline.

DOWNLOADABLE REPORT FORMS

Further Resources

BOOKS

Bullis, Amber. *Mindfulness and Food*. Minneapolis, MN: Jump!, 2020.

Carole, Bonnie. *Junk Food, Yes or No*. Vero Beach, FL: Rourke Educational Media, 2016.

Kenney, Karen Latchana. *Food Scientist*. Minneapolis, MN: Jump!, 2019.

Mattern, Joanne. *French Fries*. Hopkins, MN: Bellwether Media, 2020.

WEBSITES

FACTSURFER

Factsurfer.com gives you a safe, fun way to find more information.

1. Go to www.factsurfer.com.
2. Enter "McDonald's" into the search box and click
3. Select your book cover to see a list of related websites.

Glossary

affordable: Having a cost that is not too high; inexpensive.

brand: The name of a product made by a company.

carhop: A waiter that serves customers in their cars at a drive-in restaurant.

collector's items: Things, often rare or beautiful, that people gather and save.

curry: Indian-style spices and herbs.

fast food: Food that is prepared and sold quickly in a restaurant.

franchise: A business started legally using someone else's ideas and processes.

logo: A symbol or graphic mark that identifies a product or company.

nonprofit: An organization that is established not to make a financial gain but often works toward a social cause.

Index

PHOTO CREDITS

The images in this book are reproduced through the courtesy of: ermingut/iStockphoto, front cover (McDonald's sign), p. 31; AzriSuratmin/Shutterstock Images, front cover (hamburger, Chicken McNuggets), pp. 4, 15 (Happy Meal); Hong Vo/Shutterstock Images, front cover (breaded nuggets), p. 15 (top left); M. Unal Ozmen/ Shutterstock Images, front cover (McDonald's fries), p. 27 (McDonald's fries); Ayah Raushan/Shutterstock Images, front cover (apple pie); Nataliia K/Shutterstock Images, pp. 1, 22; foxaon1987/Shutterstock Images, p. 1 (background); Evan-Amos/CC0, pp. 3, 14; Ken Wolter/Shutterstock Images, p. 5 (top); 8th.creator/ Shutterstock Images, p. 5 (bottom); Robson90/Shutterstock Images, pp. 6-7; Featureflash Photo Agency/ Shutterstock Images, p. 8 (left); Jeffrey Mayer/Alamy Stock Photo, p. 8 (center); JStone/Shutterstock Images, p. 8 (right); Justin Sullivan/Getty Images, p. 9; Jonathan Weiss/Shutterstock Images, p. 10; Marty Lederhandler/AP Images, pp. 10-11; Bobak Ha'Eri/CC BY-SA 3.0, p. 12 (top); Public Domain, p. 12 (bottom); ATIKAN PORNCHAIPRASIT/Shutterstock Images, p. 13 (top); Toni Genes/Shutterstock, p. 13 (bottom); Sorbi/Shutterstock Images, p. 15 (top right); Keith Homan/Shutterstock Images, p. 15 (McDonald's bag); Walter Cicchetti/Shutterstock Images, pp. 16, 26 (Happy Meals); enchanted_fairy/Shutterstock Images, p. 17 (top); jfmdesign/iStockphoto, p. 17 (bottom); David Tonelson/Shutterstock Images, pp. 18-19; Robert Galan/ Shutterstock Images, p. 19; Peter Kramer/Getty Images, p. 20; Cari Rubin Photography/Shutterstock Images, p. 21; Peter Fleming/iStockphoto, pp. 22-23; Everett – Art/Shutterstock Images, p. 23; Lester Balajadia/ Shutterstock Images, p. 24 (top); Dalaifood/Shutterstock Images, p. 24 (bottom); Valentyn Volkov/Shutterstock Images, p. 25 (top); tirc83/iStockphoto, p. 25 (bottom); Aleksandr Demianiv/Shutterstock Images (top); Ayah Raushan/Shutterstock Images, p. 26 (apple pie); Tiger Images/Shutterstock Images, p. 27 (potatoes); Nattika/ Shutterstock Images, p. 27 (cut fries).

About the Author

Kaitlyn Duling has written over 100 books for children. She lives in Washington, DC.